The 5 Keys To Wellness

Written by Kelly Mather
Illustrated by Lisa Schneller

The 5 Keys To Wellness

An original production by Harmony Healing House

Published by Harmony Healing House
Lakeport, CA 95453
www.HarmonyHealingHouse.com
707-262-5005

ISBN-10: 0-9787179-8-8
ISBN-13: 978-0-9787179-8-8

The illustrations in this book were done in watercolor on Arches 140-lb. cold-press watercolor paper.
The display type and text type were set in Goudy Sans, designed by Frederic Goudy.

Printed in Canada
9 8 7 6 5 4 3 2 1

This book is dedicated to all the people who've inspired me to live healthy and helped me introduce kids to their healing ability. Love and thanks to my family: Grandma, Mom, Rick, Kacey, Julie Ann, Scotty, and Brady.

Special thanks to my Lakeside Wellness family: Bonnie, Carrie, Diane, Maura, Leslie, Tammi, Terry, and Vera.

Thanks to all who've inspired me to pursue my mission: Aleta, Chris, Doreen, Jack, Lori, Rob, Steve, Susan, Suzin, Tracy, Tom, Van, Dawn, Margaret, and Sheila.

Health Treasure

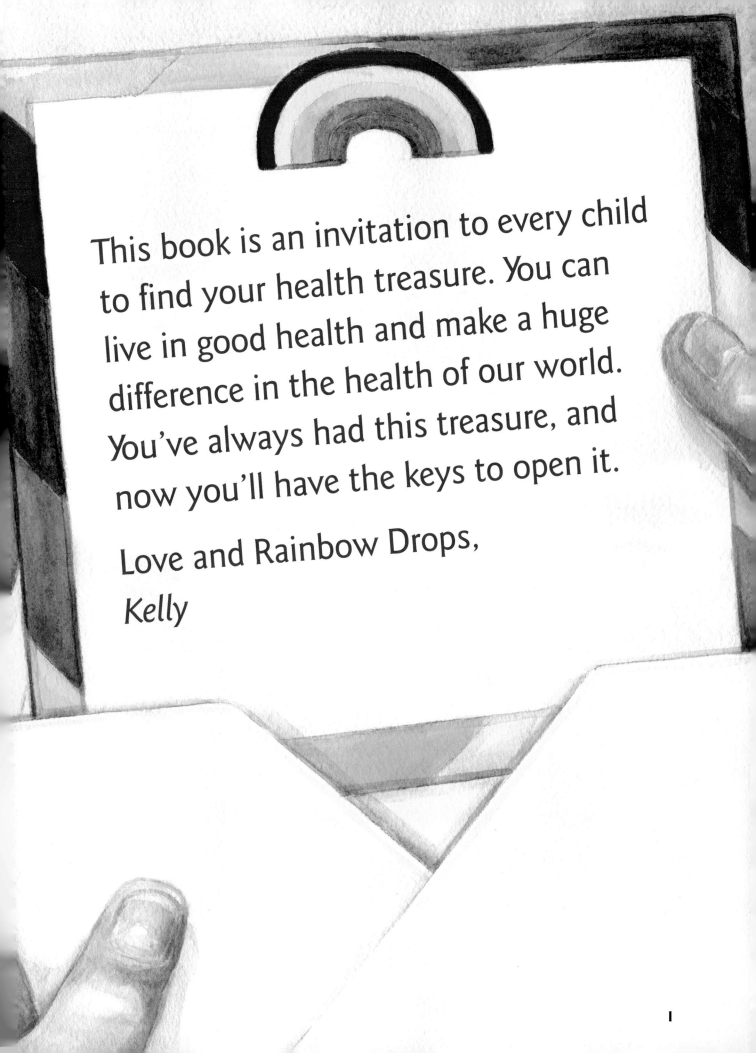

This book is an invitation to every child to find your health treasure. You can live in good health and make a huge difference in the health of our world. You've always had this treasure, and now you'll have the keys to open it.

Love and Rainbow Drops,

Kelly

Have you ever hunted for a treasure chest?
Was it locked?
Did you have the keys to open it?

The health treasure chest is like any other treasure chest. First you have to find it, and then you need the keys to open it. But this special treasure chest is locked inside of you. To find your health treasure chest, you need a wellness wheel.

WELLNESS WHEEL QUESTIONNAIRE

1 = No/Never   2 = Sometimes   3 = Usually   4 = Yes/Always

GENERAL HEALTH

1. I am well and do not get sick often.	1	2	3	4
2. I have energy and feel good all day.	1	2	3	4
3. I have little pain.	1	2	3	4
4. I don't take much medicine.	1	2	3	4
5. I wake up excited about my day.	1	2	3	4

TOTAL SCORE ____ /20

SELF LOVE

1. I like myself.	1	2	3	4
2. I appreciate my body.	1	2	3	4
3. I am usually happy and say nice things.	1	2	3	4
4. I am a good friend and have several friends.	1	2	3	4
5. I don't dwell on what others think.	1	2	3	4

TOTAL SCORE ____ /20

BREATHING

1. I do aerobic exercise 3 times a week.	1	2	3	4
2. I notice how stress affects my breathing.	1	2	3	4
3. I know how to deep breathe.	1	2	3	4
4. I take a deep breath when I'm upset.	1	2	3	4
5. I spend time outside breathing in nature daily.	1	2	3	4

TOTAL SCORE ____ /20

POSITIVE CHOICES

1. I eat 2 vegetables, 2 fruits and 2 grains every day.	1	2	3	4
2. I drink water and drink little caffeine.	1	2	3	4
3. I watch TV or play video games less than 2 hours a day.	1	2	3	4
4. My friends make me feel good.	1	2	3	4
5. I find ways to spend time that feel good.	1	2	3	4

TOTAL SCORE ____ /20

BALANCE

1. I know what I do best and do it often.	1	2	3	4
2. I take time for myself and rest daily.	1	2	3	4
3. I enjoy learning and working on projects.	1	2	3	4
4. I do creative and new activities often.	1	2	3	4
5. I play daily.	1	2	3	4

TOTAL SCORE ____ /20

TRUST

1. I trust that I can use all my experiences to learn.	1	2	3	4
2. I do not over-react.	1	2	3	4
3. I allow myself to be touched and healed as needed.	1	2	3	4
4. I am kind and find kindness is returned back to me.	1	2	3	4
5. I know my actions and thoughts affect myself and others.	1	2	3	4

TOTAL SCORE ____ /20

Chart your score on your wellness wheel.

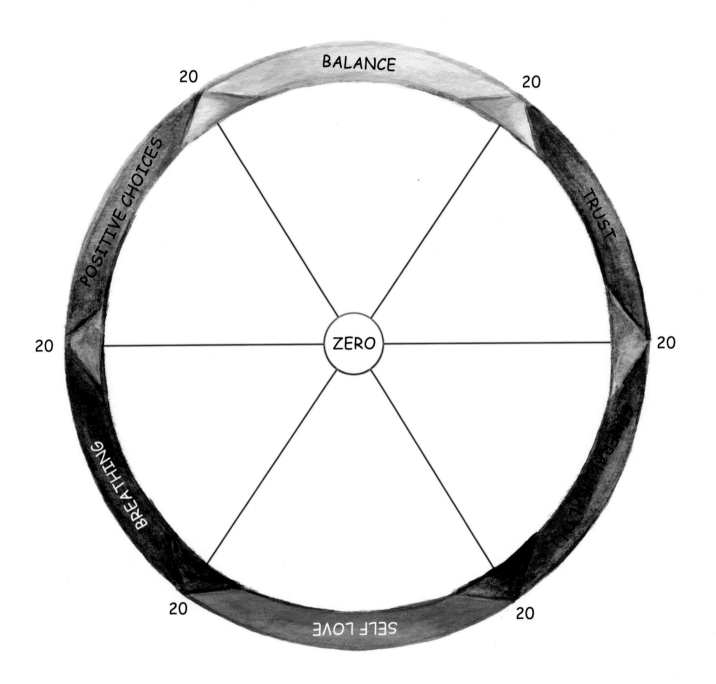

YOUR WELLNESS WHEEL

Are most parts of your wellness wheel filled in? Do you score high in a few keys to wellness and not as high in other keys? When your wheel can roll, it will roll you right to your health treasure.

You can see that this girl is fairly healthy, but she knows she could breathe better. The 5 Keys to Wellness exercises will help get the wellness wheel rolling.

The 1st Key to Wellness is Self Love

To be healthy you need to love and feel loved. The most important thing you can do for your health is to love yourself. How did you score on self-love in the wellness questionnaire?

"I scored 18 out of 20 on self-love."

"I love myself!"

Don't worry if you didn't score very high. There are lots of easy ways to love yourself. Give yourself a big hug. Look in the mirror and say, "I love you." Tell each part of your body that you love it. Say nice things about yourself. Never say mean things about yourself. Every good thing you say brings you more self-love.

"You're a good friend."

Your body is like a bucket of water. When you're born, the water in your bucket is clear and healthy. As you grow, you add things to the bucket. When you and your parents fill it with loving thoughts and words, and you surround yourself with loving people and healthful things, you'll be healthier. Fill your body bucket with love every day!

Pour out the hurtful thoughts.

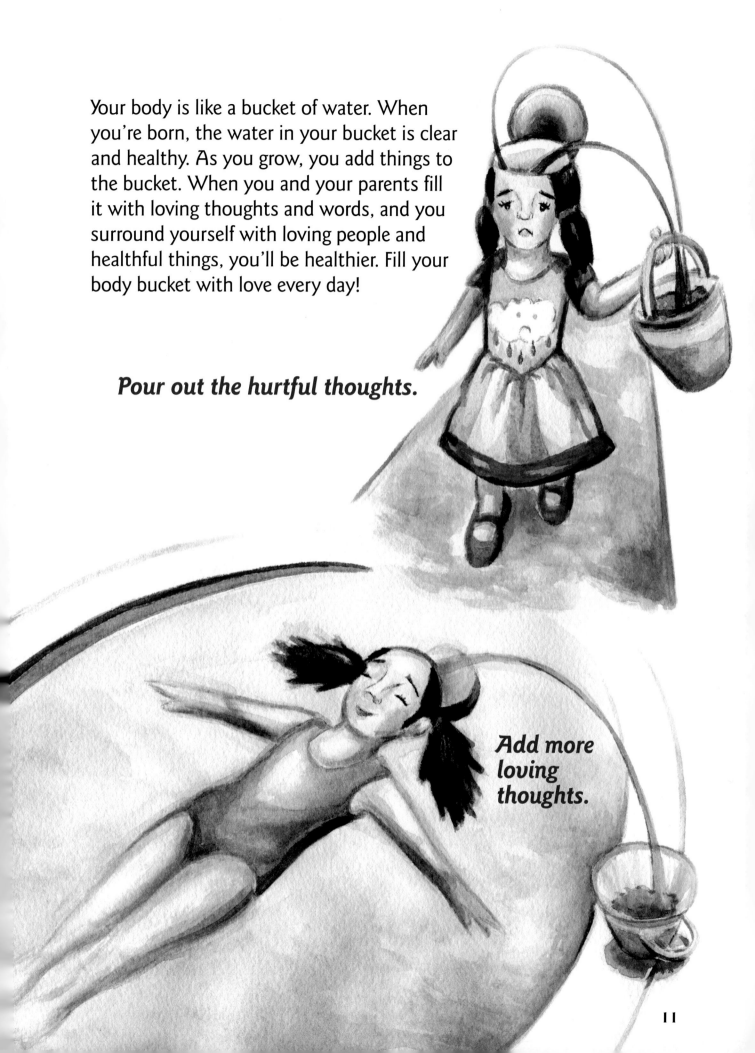

Add more loving thoughts.

If you love yourself, you don't worry about what others think. When you draw a picture, it should make you smile to see the beauty in your picture. You don't need to judge it or compare it to other people's pictures. You and your pictures are perfect and beautiful.

The way you breathe affects your health. Short, shallow breaths are unhealthy. Deep belly breaths send oxygen to every part of your body and help you feel good.

Try this deep-breathing exercise:

Count to five slowly while you inhale through your mouth as if you're sipping through a straw. Your belly will blow up like a balloon. Hold your breath for a few seconds. Then hiss the air out slowly while you count to five.

Slow, deep breathing helps your mind, body, and feelings all work together. This is called the alpha state. When you feel stressed, you might feel your breathing become shallow. In the beta state, your mind, body, and feelings work against each other. So, whatever you do, take deep breaths, and you'll find your mind, body, and feelings are supporting you! It's impossible to be stressed while you're deep breathing.

ALPHA STATE

BETA STATE

"I wanted that cookie!"

Whenever you feel upset, take a five-minute break and breathe. Spending time in nature is a great way to promote healthy breathing. After five minutes outside, you'll probably notice that your breathing is slower and you feel better right away.

"I didn't need a cookie."

The Third Key to Wellness is Making Positive Choices

Your choices can make you well or ill. You choose your food, friends, hobbies, and habits every day. If you're feeling sick, you're probably not making good choices about what you eat, what you do, and whom you spend time with.

"I have a choice? I used to think my parents made all my choices."

Here's an easy way to see if a choice is good for you.

Start with your thumb pointing sideways. Now, check how you feel. If you feel good, the way you do after you've eaten your favorite good food, or spent time with your best friend, then point your thumb up. If you feel bad, because you feel you've made an unhealthy choice, point your thumb down. The best choices give you a "thumbs-up" feeling.

"Vegetables always pass the thumb test!"

Here's another way to see if a choice is good for you.

"Smoking is weak."

"Reading is a strong choice."

Put your arm up and say your choice out loud. If your arm stays strong, it means that choice will strengthen your health. If your arm gets weak, the choice can weaken your health or make you feel sick.

If you feel angry, you have a choice. You could throw something, hit or yell at someone. Or, you could go for a run, write down your feelings, or maybe even cry. Which ones do you think are healthy choices? Healthy people have strong feelings, but they still make healthy choices.

"I always feel better when I run."

"I'm always happy when I'm helping."

Do you ever feel bored or scared or unimportant? That's the perfect time to choose to do something loving for yourself, for someone else, or for your neighborhood. This kind of choice will make you feel healthy and happy again.

The 4th Key to Wellness is Balance

Balance means doing just the right amount of everything. Each day, you work and rest and study and play. If you're feeling sick, you might be doing too much of one thing and not enough of another. Ask your parents to help you check to see if you're balancing work, play, study, and rest.

"This kind of work is fun!"

Healthy people spend time finding out what they enjoy. This means you can try a lot of new things and then ask yourself, "What do I really like to do?" What have you liked to do ever since you were little? Do you like to take care of your pets? Do you like to sing and dance? Do you like to help with the garden? Knowing what you enjoy and what you do best can lead to a job you love when you are grown up.

Try to find restful activities that refresh your energy every day. Healthy people play often, but too much play can make you feel tired all the time. And all work and too little rest can make you feel sick. We all need a little relaxation!

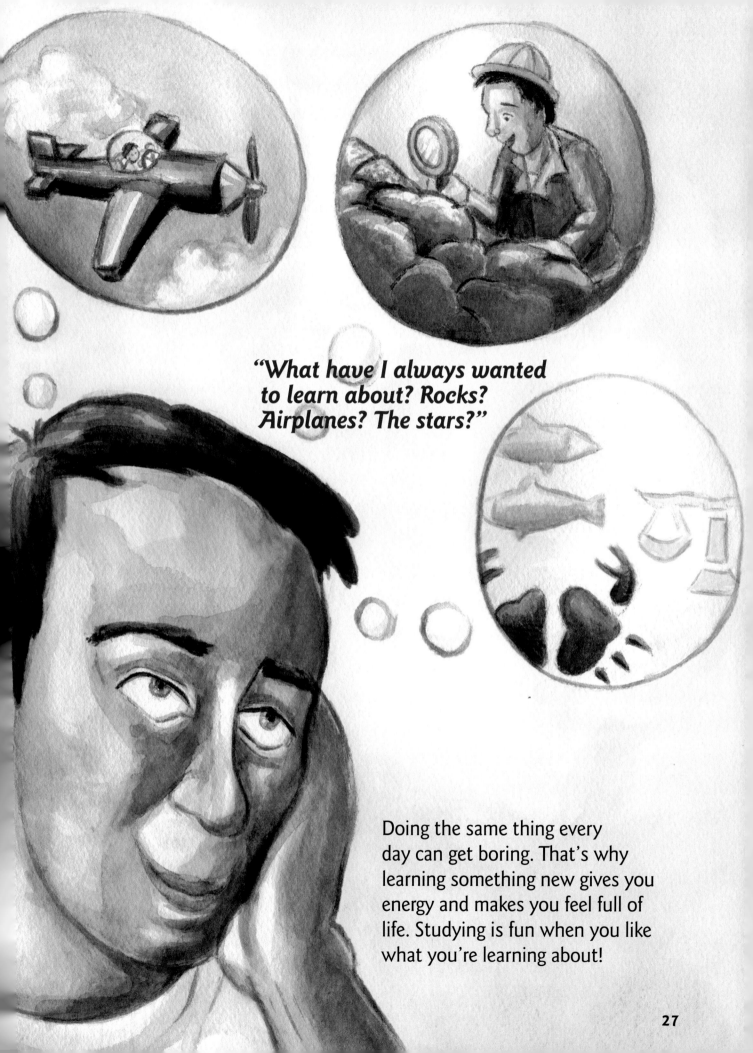

"What have I always wanted to learn about? Rocks? Airplanes? The stars?"

Doing the same thing every day can get boring. That's why learning something new gives you energy and makes you feel full of life. Studying is fun when you like what you're learning about!

"I love to bake."

"I love to ski."

"I love good movies."

You'll find many answers when you ask yourself,
"What do I do that really makes me smile?"
Healthy people play often!"

The 5th Key to Wellness is Trust

"*The accident wasn't your fault, Dad. We're okay. Everything is going to be okay.*"

Trusting is a very important key to good health. Healthy people trust that everything is okay. Worrying, being afraid, thinking about what's wrong, blaming other people or yourself, and feeling sad, angry, or guilty is a waste of energy!

You're always getting messages you can trust. All you have to do is stop and listen to them. If you feel afraid, simply stop and listen and you'll find you know just what to do.

Your body heals itself, and with your trust, it becomes well. As soon as your body is injured, it begins to heal. This miracle can always happen, and trust is the only thing you need to make it happen.

"My illness is just a reason to use every level of healing. I know my body is healing."

A way to learn trust is to apply the **Purple Rule**:
Whatever you say, whatever you do,
sooner or later comes back to you.
Try to follow this rule for at least a week.

"I started following the purple rule and good things keep happening for me."

"*I'm so glad we decided to go out on the boat. I trust you.*"

Once you trust yourself, you can trust others. We all have to rely on each other. When you trust other people, you're teaching them the keys to wellness!

Now that you have learned the 5 Keys to Wellness, you can reach the Health Treasure Chest on your complete Wellness Wheel. To reach the health treasure locked deep inside of you, you will journey through four levels of healing.

The Four Levels of Healing

First Level,
Signs of Sickness;

Second Level,
Healthy Body;

Third Level,
Healthy Thoughts
And Feelings;

Fourth Level,
Healthy Person.

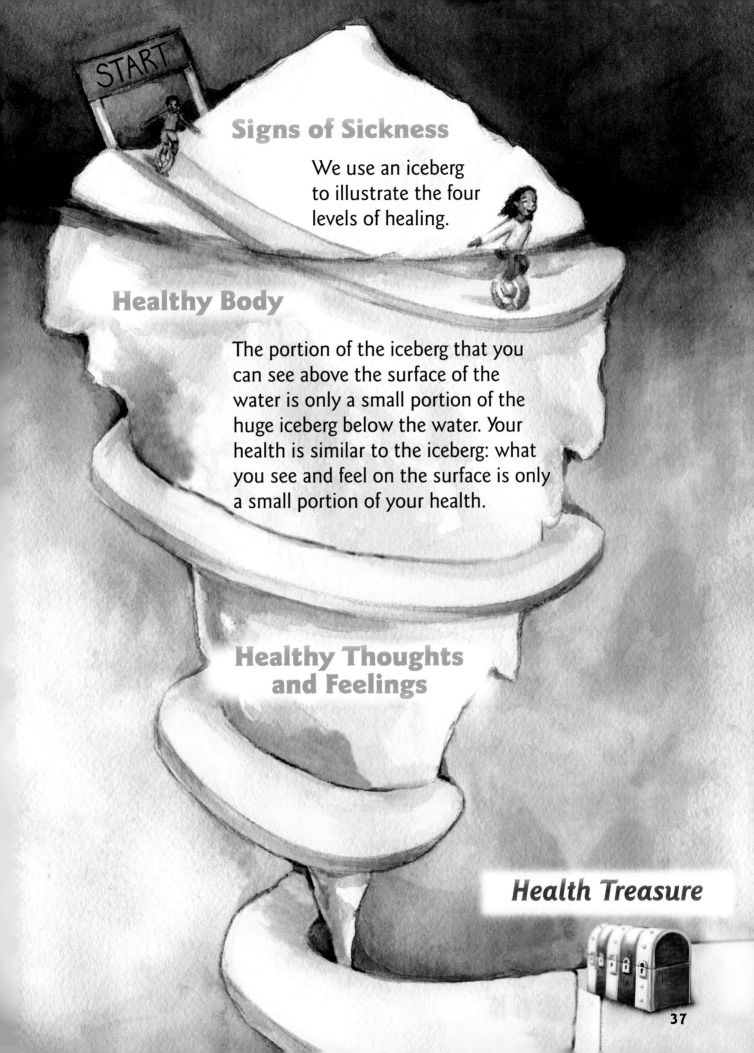

START

Signs of Sickness

We use an iceberg to illustrate the four levels of healing.

Healthy Body

The portion of the iceberg that you can see above the surface of the water is only a small portion of the huge iceberg below the water. Your health is similar to the iceberg: what you see and feel on the surface is only a small portion of your health.

Healthy Thoughts and Feelings

Health Treasure

Signs of Sickness

The first level of healing is when you have a sign of sickness. For instance, you may have a headache. Many people see a doctor when they have a sign of sickness.

"It's good that you came in to see me. You have an ear infection and that is why you have a headache."

Healthy Body

The second level of healing is when you take good care of your body. Three of the keys you just learned will help you have a healthy body: deep breathing, making positive choices, and balancing your life.

"I didn't eat any vegetables and hardly drank any water today. Maybe if I eat better, drink more water, and do some exercise, I won't get as many headaches!

What I Ate Today

Breakfast: Sugar pops and milk

Lunch: peanut butter & jelly
1 cookie
milk

Dinner:
hot dogs
macaroni & cheese
soda
chocolate cake

Healthy Thoughts and Feelings

The third level of healing is when you have healthy thoughts and feelings. The other two keys, self-love and trust, will help you.

"I'm eating better, so why did I get a headache today?" *Maybe I need to stop blaming and criticizing myself!"*

Now that you have a healthy body and healthy thoughts and feelings, you have reached the health treasure and you are a healthy person!

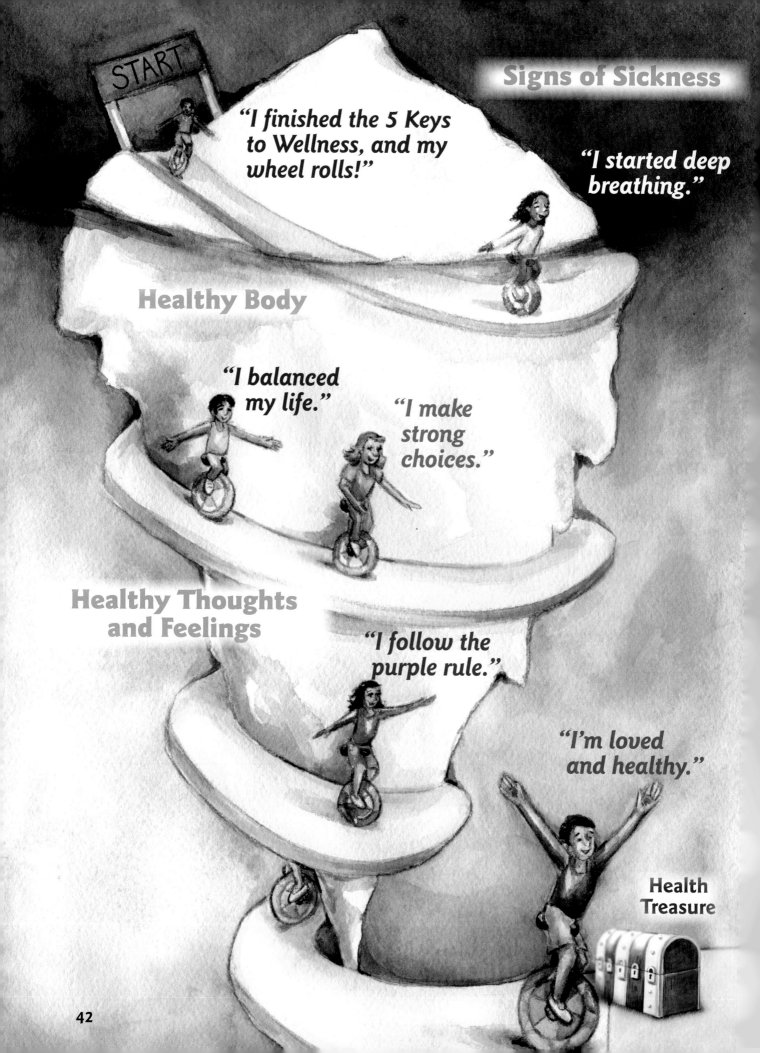

The health treasure is with you wherever you go. Simply follow the 5 Keys to Wellness and you can always be in good health. Now you can show everyone how to use The 5 Keys to Wellness to find and open their own health treasure chests.

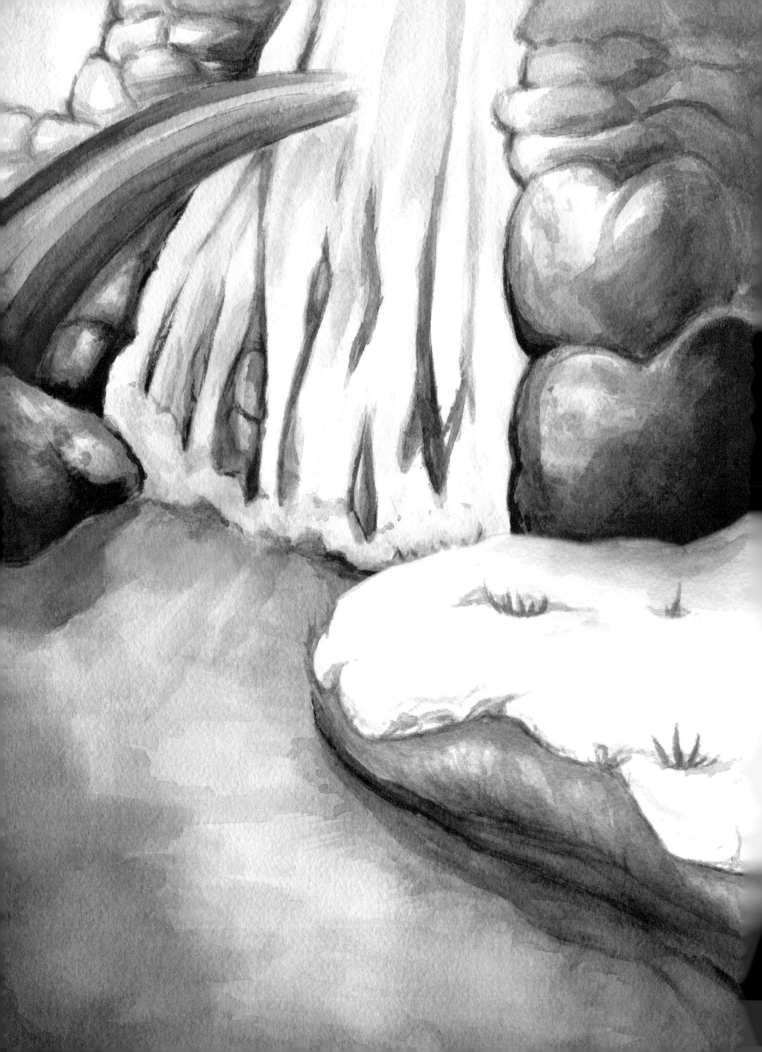